Jeepers
and
Creepers

A TALE OF TWO SISTERS

BRADLEY J. BIDELL

ISBN 978-1-63874-411-5 (paperback)
ISBN 978-1-63874-412-2 (digital)

Christian Faith Publishing, Inc.
832 Park Avenue
Meadville, PA 16335
www.christianfaithpublishing.com

Printed in the United States of America

Two Sisters and Creation

"Wachel (Ashlynn often calls her older sister this due to unrefined annunciation), gimme the block, Wachel!"

"We have to work together to build the perfect tower! Our princess needs the perfect tower for her perfect castle!"

"Hey, Jeepers and Creepers," Dad chimed in, "you two build your creation together. Nothing as large as a castle gets built by one person."

"Dad's right, Ash. Just like God used all three parts of his godhead to make the universe and everything in it, we can build the best princess tower and castle ever, if we work together!"

"Okay, sissy, let's create!"

*****

The story of creation is beautiful and awe-inspiring. To think that God created such a vast universe but only designated one planet to bear a people made in his image is truly humbling. Take some time now, parents, to read through the scripture listed above with your little one(s).

As a family, answer these questions:

1. Who is present during creation?
2. How long did creation take?
3. What order was everything created?
4. Why is God's resting on the seventh day significant?
5. Can you, like Jeepers and Creepers, work together to create something fun (whether it is with blocks or something else does not matter)?

Two Sisters and the Fall of Man

Day 2
Genesis 2:17, 3; Romans 3:23, 5:18–21

"Creepers, Mommy told us not to touch her blueberries! She's going to put you up for adoption."

"No, she's not, Wachel. I saved some bu-bewwies for her, see?"

"Oh, Ash, two blueberries do not count. Besides, she told us not to touch them at all. That's like when God told Adam and Eve not to touch or eat the fruit from the tree of the knowledge of good and evil."

"Did they eat it, Jeepers?"

"Uh, yeah! That's how sin entered the world."

"Uh-oh, I'd better put these sin berries back!"

"It's a little late now—"

*****

Jeepers swiped the last two blueberries and ran off eating them as she laughed. Creepers stood in shock for half of a second before chasing her sister, giggling.

Carefully read through Genesis 2:17 and chapter 3, along with the verses from Romans 3 and 5.

1. How did Satan present himself in the Garden of Eden?
2. Why do you think he spoke directly to Eve and not Adam or both together?
3. Why do you believe Adam did not stop Eve?
4. What was their consequence for sinning?
5. Do you get consequences when you disobey your parents?
6. In the Romans verses, who does Paul say has sinned? What is God's glory, and what is meant that we fall short of it?

Two Sisters and God's Law

Day 3
Exodus 20, 1 John 3:4–10

"Mom and Dad have rules for Creepers and me. They teach us that the rules are to help us stay out of trouble and learn right from wrong."

"Wachel, you broked the rules today!"

"What do you mean, Ashlynn?"

"You ate my chicken nuggets, and this time, Mom is going to put you up for adoption!"

Jeepers seemed taken aback, but she knew her sister was right. She had taken something that did not belong to her; she stole her sister's food.

"I'm very sorry for stealing your chicken nuggets, Creepers. Will you please forgive me?"

"Okay! I forgive you!"

*****

Creepers gave her big sister an oversized hug, and the two went off to play.

1. Do you know what God's law was called in the Old Testament?
2. What do we have now that informs us of God's rules and expectations for his children?

3. Just like our parents, God has given us commandments to follow because he loves us and desires us to live in a way that will be good for us and those around us. As you read through the passages in Exodus and 1 John, discuss with your parents:
   a. What God's laws are,
   b. How they are helpful,
   c. What your family rules are, and
   d. How you can all work together to honor God and each other.

Two Sisters and Salvation

Day 4
John 3:16–18, Acts 4:8–12

"All right, Creepers, we know how God created the world. Man disobeyed God and brought sin into the world, and God gave us laws and commandments to follow. But how do we know we are right with God?"

"I don't know. Jesus?"

"You got it! We need Jesus in our hearts as our Lord and Savior. The Bible calls it salvation."

"Jeepers, is that like when I was pwetending to drown in the living room, and you that round thing to me?"

"That was a pretend lifesaver. Yeah, Dad said salvation is like that. We are in big trouble, with no hope, and right when we think we won't make it, someone pulls us out and helps us get better!"

"Is that why Jesus died on the coss?"

"It's cross, and yes, he died to take away our sins, so we can have a relationship with God and live forever in heaven!"

"Yay! I love salvation!"

*****

We all need to realize that we need a Lord and Savior, and that, Jesus is the only one who can be both for us. Parents, challenge your children to keep in mind the fact that Jesus not only died to save us but also to be Lord over our lives as well. We will take a closer look at that later, so for now, read the passages together and discuss what salvation means to you.

1. How are we saved?
2. Who is the only one who can save us?
3. Why did God choose to give us Jesus to die for our sins?

Two Sisters and Faith

Day 5
Psalm 9:10, Proverbs 3:5, Jeremiah 29:11, Romans 15:13

"Let me tell you about the time my parents were teaching me to jump in the water."

"Oh, Jeepers, you were so scared."

"Yeah, I was definitely nervous. I wanted to make Mom and Dad proud, and Dad was right there to catch me. But even though I knew he would catch me, I was still afraid to take that first leap."

"Haha, more like fall!"

"Hush, Creepers. I knew my dad loved me and wouldn't let anything bad happen, so I did it. It got a little easier and more fun each time. That's how it is with God too. Mom says that every time we have faith and trust God, it will get a little easier and, eventually, we can face any challenge because we know that God loves us."

"I need faith just to walk into our bedroom—now that is scawy!"

Jeepers and Creepers ran off to their room; hopefully to clean it? Hey, even parents need to have faith in their children.

*****

Take some time to carefully read through these scriptures together. Faith is the foundation for a Christian's walk with Jesus. We cannot see, smell, touch, or hear him, but we know he lives in us. Despite not being able to see God, the more we obey his Word, pray, and come together as families and churches, we will see him working all around.

1. Parents, what challenges have you faced, and how has your faith helped you overcome?

2. What can your children learn from your times of trial and faith in God?
3. Children, what does faith mean to you, and how can you live it out for others to see?

Two Sisters and Priorities

Day 6
Proverbs 16:3, Matthew 6:31–34, John 3:30

"Looks like we have a lot to do today, Creepers."

"Sure do, Jeepers. Have fun!"

Rachel gave Ashlynn a stern look.

"I just kiddin'! Let's get it done before Mommy wakes up."

"Sounds good. Dad always says we have to pri...or...it...ize? Prioritize!"

"What's that?"

"He said it's getting the most important stuff done first. Like how they tell us that our relationship with Jesus is the most important part of life, so we should put him first in everything."

"Oh, so we need to pray? Dear, Jesus, please help us get our room cleaned, put away laundry, get dressed, and make coffee for Mom before she wakes up. Amen!"

"Um, we are not allowed to make coffee—"

"Oh right, Jesus, that's all you. Amen!"

"Great, now let's get the most important task done first."

The sisters looked at one another in despair and exclaimed together, "Clean our room!"

They dramatically fell to the floor and reluctantly crawl to their bedroom.

*****

As you read these verses together, pay close attention to who we are supposed to put first in our lives.

1. Why is making God our top priority so vital?
2. What happens when we do not?

3. Can you think of a time when you were not putting God above everything else?
4. What differences have you seen when you don't versus when you do?
5. How can you, as a family, make God your number one priority?

Two Sisters and Baptism

Day 7
Matthew 3:13–17, Acts 2:38, Ephesians 4:4–6

Please allow me, the author and proud dad of Jeepers and Creepers, to take this opportunity to share a personal story for this topic.

Sarah, the proud mom of Jeepers and Creepers, and I recently (July 22, 2018) had the absolute honor and privilege of witnessing our oldest daughter, Rachel (Jeepers), publicly declare her faith and salvation in Jesus through the act of water baptism. As tears welled up in my eyes, all I could do was praise God, pray for her faith to grow, and pray for her sister, Ashlynn, to do the same someday. Although water baptism has been debated as being essential for salvation, one thing we can all agree on is that even our Lord humbled himself to be publicly baptized, as his commitment to honor and obey the Father, and it is always a joyous and beautiful occasion when a loved one (especially our own children) follows in the footsteps of Christ.

Parents, I strongly implore you to read these scripture passages and even look up others together and discuss the importance and significance of proclaiming that the old sinful nature is gone and the new life in Jesus has begun.

1. Have your children been baptized?
2. If so, what were their thoughts and feelings?
3. What are they doing to grow in their relationship with Jesus?
4. If they have not been baptized, do they understand what it symbolizes and why it is important in a Christian's life?
5. Do they believe they are ready to be baptized?

I hope this promotes some heartfelt, meaningful conversation. With that, I turn it back over to my girls!

Two Sisters and Prayer

Day 8
Daniel 9:18, Philippians 4:6–7, James 5:16

"Wachel, it's time for bed."

"Right, and you know what that means, Creepers?"

"Bedtime prayers?"

"Exactly! Mom and Dad say that prayer is how we talk to God."

"Well, Jeepers, I've been talking to God all day, asking him to not let Dad find the gummies I stashed in the couch for tomorrow."

"Oh boy,"—Jeepers gave her sister an overdramatic eye roll—"C'mon Creepers, I'll pray for your protection."

"Woohoo! Let's go pray, sister!"

*****

Prayer is our direct line to God, through the Holy Spirit. It is just like carrying a conversation with anyone; speaking and listening. God speaks to us, his children, in many different ways—primarily through his Word (the Bible).

Prayer is also one of the most powerful tools a Christian has when it comes to living a life that is right with God. When we are in trouble, we can ask for wisdom and strength. When we see someone in need, we can pray for God to bless them (and we should help them if we can). When someone says they do not believe in God, we should pray for their salvation.

I have found prayer especially useful when dealing with someone who seems difficult to handle. Usually what happens is God allows me to see that person through his eyes and allows me to love them the way he does. One of the most important things for us to pray for is our own salvation, forgiveness from sin, and continual spiritual growth.

Read the verses together and then find others about prayer. Close this reading by going around a circle and praying for each other.

Two Sisters and Forgiveness

Day 9
Genesis 45:1–15, Matthew 6:14–15, Colossians 3:12–14

"Uh-oh—"

"What happened, Creepers?"

"I accidentally ripped your teddy bear, Jeepers."

"Ugh! Why would you do that?"

"I'm sowwy, Wachel."

Their mom interjected from the next room, "Rachel, remember what we taught you about forgiveness."

"Okay, Mom. I forgive you, Ash. It's just a toy, not the end of the world, like Dad says."

"Thank you, sister! Now come here so I can give you a biiiiig hug!"

Jeepers jokingly ran away with her little sister chasing with open arms.

*****

Forgiveness is the letting go of a wrong done by someone else and never again holding it against them. Whether that wrong was done intentionally or accidentally, God is very clear that we are to forgive that person. He even went so far as to say that if we do not forgive others, he will not forgive us of our sins.

I don't know about you, but I want God to forgive me, and holding a grudge or bitterness against someone is not worth not having my own sins forgiven. Forgiveness is taken very seriously in the Bible; it can be one of the most freeing experiences we can have. What I mean is that when we forgive others, we are trusting God to take care of the situation, and we are showing God that we understand he is in control and how much he has forgiven us.

As you read through these verses together, discuss how you have dealt with forgiveness.

Have you seen how forgiveness frees you to love the person who wronged you?

Have you ever struggled to forgive someone (including yourself)?

How did that affect your relationship with Jesus?

How did it affect your relationship with the other individual(s)?

Parents, do you need each other or your children for something?

Children, do you need to forgive your siblings or your parents for something?

I challenge you to forgive everyone you believe has genuinely wronged or hurt you and watch how God transforms your heart. I've done it, and it is the most liberating experience in the world!

Two Sisters and Church

Day 10
Deuteronomy 31:12–13, Acts 2:42–46, Hebrews 10:24–25

"Wachel, wake up, it's Sunday!"

"Alright, Ash, I get it. It's time to get ready for church."

"Mommy picked out our dresses last night, but daddy wants us to wait till after breakfast to put them on."

"I like getting dressed up for church because I feel like I'm giving my best to God."

"Yeah, I like being with all the people who love Jesus, and I like going to Sunday school."

"Church is great for a lot of reasons, and God loves when we get together with other Christians. Let's go. Jeepers and Creepers, away!"

*****

Jeepers and Creepers really do love going to church every week. Their mom and I are thrilled about that, as it has always been an important part of our lives as well.

1. How about you? Does your family attend a Bible church (one that teaches the Bible as God's absolute truth) regularly?
2. What are your favorite parts about church?
3. Based on the passages, do you believe God cares if we go to church?

Church is much more than just a physical building; it is a gathering of people who believe that the God of the Bible is the one true God. They get together, therefore, to pray, sing songs of worship and praise, give a portion back to God of what he has given them to support the efforts of ministry, learn from God's Word, and encourage one another in their faith. It is also important that we invite family and friends, who currently do not have a relationship with Jesus, to church. This is a great way for them to see the difference God makes in people's lives, and that, they, too, can have a relationship with him through Jesus.

Who do you know that you could invite to church?

Work together as a family to implement "each one, reach one" and get people to church!

Two Sisters and Worship

Day 11
Psalm 95, 1 Chronicles 16:23–31, Hebrews
12:28–29, Romans 12:1–2

"Hey, Creepers, what's your favorite part of a church service?"

"Um, I like when we get to eat bread and dwink grape juice. Yum!"

"That's called communion, but we don't do that every Sunday."

"Oh well, I love singing!"

"Worship is my favorite too. Why don't we go sing a song to Mom, right now!?"

"Woohoo! We're gonna sing to Mommy!"

They scurried off to grace their mom with what could only have been their version of a worship song.

*****

Most churches include a time in their services for singing songs to God. This is typically known as worship time or worship hour (despite not actually lasting that long). The Bible teaches us that we are to come together and sing spiritual songs, hymns, and praises. We also worship God in what we do and how we live our lives.

1. What does worship mean to you?
2. Why do we worship God?
3. Besides music and song, how else do we worship God?

As you read the verses, talk about your favorite worship and praise songs. This might be an excellent time to sing a couple as a family, and don't worry, God doesn't necessarily care if we can carry a tune, so long as it comes from the heart.

Two Sisters and Communion

Day 12
Exodus 25:30, Matthew 26:26–28, 1 Corinthians 11:23–29

"Hey, Creepers, remember when you told me you like eating bread and drinking juice at church?"

"I remember, Jeepers."

"You are in luck because communion is this Sunday!"

"Woohoo! I love com-oo-nin!"

"It's communion, and so do I. But Mommy and Daddy say we can't take it unless we have asked Jesus to forgive our sins."

"Oh, sissy, you better start prayin' 'cuz I heard you call me a bad name."

"Nuh-uh, you called me a bad name."

Creepers's jaw practically hit the floor, and with her eyes wide and hands over her heart, she twirled down to the ground. The sisters shared a laugh and went to play.

*****

Communion is one of the most important acts in a Christian's life because it is ordered by God to remember and honor Jesus for giving his life for our sins on the cross. Jesus led the very first communion with his disciples and a handful of close followers in the hours leading to his betrayal, arrest, trial, and crucifixion. He was very clear on what the bread and wine (or juice for us) symbolizes and why it is so important for believers to continue this tradition until his return to earth. We know from these verses that the bread, which was broken to give thanks, represents Jesus's body, which was broken through flogging and the entire crucifixion process. Likewise,

20

we know that the wine/juice is a symbol of the precious, perfect blood that Jesus allowed to be shed for the washing away of our sins.

1. Does your church practice communion?
2. Do you examine your heart and get right with God prior to taking it?
3. Why is communion so important?

Parents, take time to discuss with your children why we take communion and why it is so significant.

Two Sisters and Tithe

Day 13
Proverbs 3:9–10, Mark 12:41–44

"Hey, Creepers, do you still have that dollar Mom gave you?"

"Oh yes, Jeepers! I'm gonna put it in the offers at church."

"You mean the offering. Dad says it's called tithing. He said we should always give God the first portion of our earnings as a way of thanking him for providing and as a sign of our faith that he will continue to provide."

"Didn't Dad also say something about stewart?"

"Steward," Dad called from the kitchen.

"Thanks, Daddy. Yeah, steward's ship!"

"Stewardship!" Dad called out again.

Jeepers and Creepers just rolled their eyes and laughed as they scampered off to play outside.

*****

Tithing is the giving of a portion of our income as a dedication back to God. The Bible says that everything in the world is God's because he created it. Basically everything in our lives is what you might say "on loan" from God. This goes beyond just our income and includes our family, food, clothing, jobs, and so on; it all belongs to God, and he has allowed us to become stewards of all of these things.

A steward is simply one who is entrusted to manage or take care of something on behalf of the owner. Being a good steward means we must use all of our time, resources, gifts, and talents (yes, our talents and skills are areas of stewardship as well) in a way that will (1) glorify God, (2) bless others, and (3) help to further the ministry of the good news of Jesus (ministry).

Tithing, as stated by Jeepers, is one way we show God that we are thankful and trust him to continue to meet all of our physical, earthly needs.

Read the verses and discuss the importance of tithing and stewardship.

1. Parents, are you tithing and teaching your children to tithe? This might be a great opportunity to go over your budget as a family and make sure that tithe and offerings are at the top of the list (plus it's great for kids to see the importance of a budget).
2. What other ways can you be a good steward of your time, resources, job, school work, talents, and so on?

Two Sisters Set Apart

Day 14
Genesis 12:1–2, 2; Corinthians 6:14–17; 1 John 2:15

"Hey, Jeepers, I saw you playing with that kid on the playground. Nobody else wanted to play with him."

"Yeah, other kids were being pretty mean to him, but Mom and Dad taught us that as Christians, we have to be different."

"Oh, you are different, hahaha. But I know I don't like when people are mean to me. Good job, sissy!"

"Thanks, Ash. I know Jesus was nice to a lot of people who were treated badly by others, so I want to do the same. Dad said that the Bible tells us to be holy, like God."

This statement received a look of shock and despair from Rachel's little sister, who had no intention of putting holes in herself.

"Don't worry, Creepers, holy doesn't mean we walk around with holes in our bodies. It means we are supposed to not sin but be loving and truthful to other people."

"Whew! I was scared for a minute! Hahaha!"

Everyone got a good laugh as the four drove away from the park.

*****

Just like God called Abram and his wife, Sarai, out of their homeland, to set them apart for his purpose, he calls us, as Christians, out from among the unsaved world. So what does this mean? Are we not to have contact with unbelievers? That would be impossible as Paul said, unless we physically leave the world.

In my observations of Christian lives, it seems as though many Christians go to one extreme or the other. Either they pay no attention to this portion of scripture and continue to act like people who do not have Jesus as their Lord and Savior or they do try to completely alienate and isolate themselves from the rest of the population. One side says, "Show me in the Bible where it says I cannot do this. It's not sin," while the other side tends to believe that any interaction with unbelievers is not holding themselves to God's standard for holiness.

What is holy? Holy means "to be set apart, to be different," and God is very clear that we are to "be holy as I am holy."

As you read and discuss these verses, pay close attention to the passage in 2 Corinthians. So many people seem to overuse these verses regarding marriage, and while that is okay and true, Paul is not even talking about marriage here; he is referring to the believers life in general and not engaging in sinful activity or spending too much time with unbelievers.

1. What does holiness look like to you?
2. How can your family establish a standard of holiness within your home?
3. What can you do to be an example of holiness to others, while still showing them the love and grace of Jesus?

I would urge you to lovingly hold each other in your family accountable to a standard of holiness that brings honor and glory to God.

Two Sisters and Truth

Day 15
Proverbs 12:19–22, John 8:32, John 14:6

"Creepers, did you take my doll?"

"No, Jeepers, I didn't take anything."

"Then why is it missing? It was on my shelf last night."

"Maybe Mommy took it?"

Mom called from another room, "Don't bring me into your lie, Ashlynn."

"Aha! I knew you were lying."

"I'm sowwy, Wachel. I took your dolly, so I could dress her up for you, see?"

"Oh my. Next time, just tell the truth. It is, after all, what sets us free."

The sisters continued playing together with their dolls and other toys, and both learned the value of telling the truth.

*****

We know that God's Word is absolute truth because God is incapable of lying.

Absolute means that everything in the Bible is real and trustworthy. Just as God is all truth, he also expects and requires us to not only tell the truth but to be honest in everything we do. We can call this integrity, living in according to God's truth in every aspect of life. We do this whether people see it or not because God always knows our thoughts, desires, words, and actions.

Children, did you know that obeying your parents even when they are not around is part of living a true life of integrity? Feel free to look up other verses regarding telling and living in truth. Jesus called himself the truth, and that means if we live according to his examples, we are living in truth.

1. Why is truth so important?
2. Have you seen how lying hurts others and can strain your relationship with them?
3. What is meant by "the truth will set you free"?
4. How can your family live in God's truth and Christlike integrity?

Two Sisters and Rivalry

Day 16
Genesis 37, Luke 15:11–32, Philippians 2:3–4

"Hey, Jeepers. I'm Mommy and Daddy's favowit child!"

"Why do you say that, Creepers?"

"'Cause they like me more."

"What makes you think they like you more?"

"They gived me ice cream when you were at school."

"So? They gave me ice cream when I got home."

Dad chimed in, "You two know that we like and love you equally, just like God loves his children all the same."

They replied in unison, "Okay, Dad!"

*****

Sometimes we think our parents favor or love one child more than us (unless of course you are an only child). Most likely, this is not true and is probably caused by insecurities we need to bring to God and or a wrong/weak view of who we are in Christ Jesus and how he sees us. It is understandable why Joseph's brothers believed he was Jacob's favorite son, but God does not desire rivalry between siblings, and parents need to be careful how we interact with our children.

1. Was Jacob wrong for singling out Joseph with the gift of the coat?
2. Did Jacob intentionally upset his other sons?

When we read the whole story, we understand that God allowed the brothers to act out in jealousy because it eventually got Joseph exactly where God wanted him. His brothers came to realize how wrong they were and repented for their sin against him.

1. Let's look at the prodigal son in Luke 15.
2. Did he realize his identity as a son and an heir to his father's wealth?
3. Was his brother justified for complaining about the celebration their dad threw upon his lost brother's return?
4. How do you think God feels when we become jealous over our siblings, both biological and spiritual (we are all brothers and sisters in Christ)?
5. Can you think of a time when you experienced jealousy or rivalry with someone close to you?
6. Was it worth getting mad or upset?
7. How can we, as families, work together to eliminate rivalry?

Let's esteem each other as better than ourselves, put the needs of others first, and rejoice when good things happen to others, especially our own siblings and family members.

Two Sisters and Sharing

Day 17
Isaiah 58:7, Acts 4:32–35

"Boy, that cookie looks delicious, Creepers."

"Mmm, it is, Jeepers! Yum, yum in my tum tum!"

"Are there more?"

"Nope, last one!"

Rachel's face was overtaken by sadness.

"Ya' know what, sissy? Mom told me that God likes when we share, so here you go."

Ashlynn broke the cookie in half and watched the joy come back to her sister's face.

"Aw, thank you, little sister. That's very thoughtful and kind of you."

"You're welcome. Now let's get some milk. These cookies are thirsty!"

They laughed as they ran to the kitchen to wash the cookies down with a cup of cold milk!

*****

Being a Christian is not about keeping everything to ourselves. We need to recognize that all we have is a blessing and a gift from God.

I remember a time when I did not have a place to call home, and God had a wonderful couple take me in. One night, I was sitting by a small fire, talking with the husband, and he reassured me that I could make myself at home because none of it was theirs anyway. He knew that everything they had in their lives and in their home was God's provision for them, to be used to bless others.

As you read the verses in Isaiah and Acts, you will see that these folks understood the same truth. In fact, loving-kindness/mercy (acts of love and sharing) are throughout the Bible. Maybe you, as a family, can find a few more right now.

1. Why is it important to view our possessions, time, money, and talents as God's and not ours?
2. Does it please God when we give to those in need?
3. If we are able, should we help others?
4. How might someone be affected by our acts of sharing and loving-kindness?
5. What can you, as a family, do to help others know Jesus through sharing?

Two Sisters and Obedience

Day 18
Deuteronomy 11:1, Proverbs 22:6,
Galatians 6:1–3, Colossians 3:20

"Jeepers, come jump on Mommy and Daddy's bed with me!"

"Creepers, you know we are not supposed to be in their room, and we are definitely not allowed to jump on their bed."

"Aw c'mon, sissy, it's fun! I won't tell them."

"That doesn't matter, Ash. Remember, Dad says that children are supposed to obey their parents because that means we are also obeying God."

Ashlynn dropped to her knees and crawled off the bed.

"In that case, I'm gonna obey! Now let's go jump on Mom and Dad instead!"

They scampered off to gang up on their un-expecting parents.

*****

Laws are meant to be obeyed and are in place to protect people from harm. The Bible is God's law for us who believe and have faith in him and is designed in a way that, when followed, will be a blessing to us and others. God's laws and commands are not meant to restrict or hold us back. On the contrary, every ordinance from God was created to help us live a free and full life in Jesus.

God has placed several people in authority over us. Some include parents, teachers, pastors, supervisors, and government. As long as what these authority figures are telling us to do are right in God's eyes, it is our responsibility and pleasure, as Christians, to obey and honor them.

As you read and discuss these verses, think about the importance of obedience.

1. Why does God want us to obey rather than doing what we desire?
2. As our parents have consequences for disobedience, God also administers consequences; what are some?
3. Think of a time when you disobeyed someone in authority.
    a. How did you feel?
    b. How did it make the other person feel?

As a family, come up with some basic rules and expectations for everyone and discuss how you can all follow them; encourage one another. Each day, ask yourself if what you are doing is in obedience to God and the authorities he has placed over you.

Two Sisters and Helping

Day 19
Exodus 17:12, Ecclesiastes 4:9–10, Luke 6:38; Galatians 6:2

"What are you doing, Jeepers?"

"Picking up our room, like Mom asked."

"You want help?"

"Well, Creepers, it is your room too."

"Hmmm, good point. I guess I could help—"

"Oh my, that's soooo kind of you!"

Ashlynn got a big grin and shrugged her shoulders.

"Like Daddy says [in her best dad voice], I do what I can."

This was met by the biggest eye roll ever, and the sisters laughed as they carried on cleaning their room together.

*****

Remember the story of Adam and Eve? God created Eve to be a helpmate to Adam. God not only knew that life would be better with someone, but he also knew there was a lot to be done in Eden, and one person could not handle it.

We are not designed to walk through life alone, and we certainly cannot get everything done by ourselves. Our Father designed us to work together and help one another. These verses talk about the importance of working together. The verse in Luke even states (as spoken by Christ) that when we do things for others, it will come back to us.

When Moses was interceding for Israel's victory, when was it that they were successful? (Hint: this is the passage in Exodus 17). Paul says, in his letter to the church in Galatia, that we are fulfilling God's law when we "ear each other's burdens."

1. What does it mean to bear someone's burdens?

2. Why is this so important to God, and why should we take it seriously?
3. Have you ever been in need, with nobody to help you?
4. How did that make you feel?
5. Have you ever been helped or helped someone else in need?
6. What difference did that make in your life?
7. In their lives? What would life be like if everyone just stuck to themselves, and nobody cared to help those in need?
8. What can you, as a family, do to help each other, and how can you help those around you—neighbors, other family members, peers, coworkers, and so on?

Once we realize and embrace the fact that life is so much bigger than ourselves and that God desires us to help others, I promise you, life will start to become more fulfilling, joyful, and complete.

Two Sisters and Family

Day 20
Proverbs 23:22, Malachi 2:16, Matthew
19:4–6, Ephesians 5:22–6:9

"Jeepers, you are my bestest, most favowit sister *ever!*"

Ashlynn dramatically embraced Rachel. "Um, Creepers, I'm your only sister."

Letting go of her sister, Creepers responded with eyes wide and an oversized grin, "Then I guess you don't have much competition!"

"Nope, and that's good because we are stuck as sisters for life."

"Even worse, Mommy and Daddy are stuck with both of us for life!"

"They don't mind. Daddy says our family is exactly how God wants it, and I love our family just the way it is."

"Me too! Now where are those bestest parents of ours?"

The sisters hurried away to find their bestest and only parents.

*****

Family is God's design. He created men and women to be paired together as husband and wife and to raise children together. It's not that God was lonely or needed someone to worship him. He created people to share his love with and families to be an example of his truth and love to others.

Each member of the family has a specific role, as you will see in these verses and any others you look up together.

Men, we have the greatest responsibility of any family member—to lead, serve, protect, and provide for our wives and children. Sadly I admit I have not always been very good at this, and I am still learning and growing.

It is God's will for each member to work together in truth, love, and unity and to show the rest of the world how Christ loves the church. Our heavenly Father takes marriage and family extremely seriously, so we should as well.

1. Why do you think God hates divorce?
2. Does it bother you that so many Christian homes are just as broken and divided as those who do not know Jesus? It bothers me, which is why my wife and I decided to fight for our marriage and family; even after being divorced for over a year. Most of us probably know couples on their second marriages who agree that they wish things had gone differently with their first. This is why it is so important for each family member to know and embrace their God-given roles and work together to make their families thrive.
3. What is your role and how can your family work together to fulfill God's purpose for the Christian family?

Two Sisters and Witnessing

Day 21
Isaiah 6:8, Matthew 28:18–20, Revelation 12:11

Jeepers walked in on Creepers talking to her stuffed animals, which she had lined up on her bed.

"What'cha doin', Creepers?"

"Hi, Jeepers, I'm telling these animals about Jesus. They need to be saved."

"You're witnessing to your toys?"

"No, I'm evan-gizing!"

"You mean evangelizing. They are the same thing. Dad said that witnessing and evangelizing are when we tell others about how Jesus died on the cross for their sins."

"Yep, I'm evan-gizing and witnessing. They are really naughty, so they need both."

Rachel thumped her palm to her forehead, "Oh brother—"

"You need Jesus, and you definitely need Jesus, Mr. Bear!"

Ashlynn carried on with her bedroom revival, as Rachel shook her head and walked away.

*****

Even before Jesus walked the earth, God used people, called prophets, to foretell of his coming. As we read through the accounts in the gospels (Matthew, Mark, Luke, and John), we see that Jesus sent out disciples two-by-two to go into surrounding towns and cities to preach repentance (turning from sin/self to God), "for the Kingdom of God is at hand" (Matthew 4:17). In other words, this Jesus, this Son of God that had long been prophesied was finally here on earth, and people should turn away from their sin and give their lives to God.

After Jesus was crucified and raised from the dead, he spent time with his disciples and gave them the command to go into the world and make more disciples (followers of Christ). We also bare that responsibility today.

In today's scripture reading,

1. Why was Isaiah so excited and ready to go tell Israel about the coming Messiah?
2. Why did his mouth need to be purified first?
3. Why does God want us to tell others about salvation through Jesus?

Who are the people in your life that you can and should share Jesus with?

Keep in mind, there is no such thing as separation of church and state with God, so don't be afraid to talk about God at school, the workplace, or anywhere. I remember times of going out in groups and talking with strangers about the gospel of Christ. Those have been some of the most fulfilling times as a believer.

Discuss ways your family can tell others about Jesus, even if you have to practice on stuffed animals first.

Two Sisters and Worrying

Day 22
Psalm 55:22, Proverbs 12:25, Matthew
6:25–34, Philippians 4:4–7

Creepers noticed her sister on the couch, sitting with her knees to her chin, arms wrapped around them, and her face expressionless.

"What's wrong, Jeepers?"

"I'm worried, Creepers."

"What are you worried about?"

"Grandma. She is having her surgery today."

"Oh yeah, but Mommy said it's not serious and that gwandma will be just fine, so nothing to worry about, kid!"

A smile came over Rachel, "You're right. Besides, she has Jesus in her, and he says we have nothing to worry about! Thanks for the encouragement, little sister."

"Anytime, sissy! Besides, you're the one who is always reassuring me. This was my chance to help you! I love you, Jeepers."

"I love you, too, Creepers. Let's pray for Grandma and trust God to take care of her."

The sisters knelt down and prayed together for their grandmother.

*****

Why do we worry? Think about that—we have Almighty God who created the universe and everything in it, dwelling in us, yet we dare to question his ability to get us through our circumstances.

Despite being guilty of this myself, when I think about it, it really does not make sense. If God can control and balance everything in the entire universe simultaneously, why wouldn't he be more than able to be in control of my situation?

In Matthew, Jesus says, "Do not worry." This is a command, not a suggestion. He did not say, "Well, try not to worry, but it's okay, I understand if you do." No, he plainly stated, "Do not worry." To me, this would imply that by worrying, we are actually denying God's ability to take care of us, and this is thus a sin.

Paul says in his letter to the Philippians not to worry or be anxious about anything. There is absolutely nothing we should worry about when we have the Spirit of God dwelling in us. When we give our worries and anxious thoughts to God, he will grant us his peace—a peace that is even greater than knowledge that we cannot understand (Philippians 4).

1. What are you worried about in your life?
2. Do you believe God is bigger than your problems and will take care of you?
3. What would your life look like if you let go and let God?

Take this time to discuss, as a family, what you have been worrying about, and repent as needed for the things you have not trusted God with. Each day, encourage each other and remind each other that you have nothing to worry about because God is in control.

Two Sisters and Sorrow

Day 23
Psalm 34:18, Matthew 5:4, John 14:1, Revelation 21:4

"This is sad, Creepers."

"What is, Jeepers?"

"Mommy is not feeling well and is having a bad day."

"Oh no, that is sad. What should we do?"

"Well, Dad says that God will comfort those who are sad. Mom needs God's comfort."

"So we should pray for Mommy?"

"Absolutely! Let's ask God to heal her and comfort her."

Jeepers and Creepers went to their mom and prayed for her, and then, they brought her a cookie, hoping it would cheer her up.

*****

Sorrow is defined by dictionary.com as "distress caused by loss, affliction, disappointment, grief, sadness, or regret."

There are a number of factors that trigger sorrow in our lives. Some include the death of a loved one, personal sickness, the loss of a job, getting a bad grade in school, losing in a sport, and so on. Thankfully the Bible, as we see from the readings above, is very clear that God wants to be our comfort. This means he not only desires to heal our broken hearts but he wants to be the very thing that heals it. I'm not saying that God won't bring someone along to comfort us, but ultimately, our peace, comfort, and joy is God.

We are not to dwell in our sorrows. God wants us to come to him and completely surrender them to him. That is not to say that our problems will instantly go away or that we will instantly feel the sorrow and pain leave. We do not live by feelings but by faith, so when we give our sorrow to God, he instantly comes alongside of us, and as we trust in him, he will bring us through in his time and way.

Is there sorrow in your life?

Do you believe that God will wipe away your tears and come close to you?

How can you let go of your sorrow and pain and allow God to be the fulfillment of your joy?

How can you, as a family, join together and bear each other's sorrow and allow God to heal the pain in your family?

I know it's not easy in the moment, but if we give our sorrow to God every day, he will fulfill his promise to come close to us and wipe away our tears.

Two Sisters and Fear

Day 24
Joshua 1:3–9, Isaiah 43:1–10, 2 Timothy 1:7, 1 John 4:18

"Hey, Jeepers, are you excited to start school?"

"I'm mostly excited, Creepers, but I'm a little afraid."

"What are you afraid of?"

"I don't know. What if I don't know what to do? Or what if the other kids don't like me? What if I don't do well?"

"Oh, sissy, you don't have to be afraid. Mommy says we have nothing to fear when we have Jesus."

"That's true. Thanks for that encouragement, Ash."

"Of course, Wachel! Remember, you are my bestest, most favowit sister!"

Ashlynn stretched out her arms, and Rachel laughed as she ran from her sister's attempt to shower her in hugs and kisses.

*****

I firmly believe that when we fear something, it's because we do not understand it. This is a great opportunity for us to trust God, as he understands everything in the physical and spiritual realm because he created it all. Therefore, there is no fear in God. In fact, God commanded Joshua not to be afraid or discouraged. He gave the same command to Isaiah and gives us the very same command today. By this standard, it seems as though fear is not of God and is, therefore, sin if we remain in it.

When we fear, we are not trusting God to protect and take care of us. As a matter of fact, God has given us his Spirit of power, not fear (1 Timothy 1), and John stated that "perfect love casts out all fear." In other words, because God is love, there is absolutely no fear in him, and we who love him have absolutely no reason to fear. God is with us. He lives in us. We need to walk in his power and courage.

1. Is there something in your life that you are in fear of?
2. Can you think of a time when you feared something but trusted God to overcome it?
3. What was the difference between a time you trusted versus a time when you allowed fear to overcome you?

As a family, share your own thoughts on what fear is and how you can live in God's courage and strength.

Two Sisters and Death

Day 25
*Isaiah 57:1–2, Ecclesiastes 7:1, 1 Thessalonians
4:13–14, Hebrews 9:27–28*

Jeepers and Creepers sat silently in the car as Dad drove from state to state. Finally, Creepers looked at her sister and said, "What's wrong with Aunt C?"

"She is dying."

"Oh no, that's so sad."

"Yes, it is. We are going out there to say goodbye to her before God brings her home."

"God has a home for Aunt C?"

"Yes, she lived a life of faith in Jesus and trusted him as her Lord and Savior, so she's going to be with God in heaven."

"Yay, that's great news!"

"It is, but unfortunately, not everyone goes to heaven when they die. People who do not put their trust in Jesus will be separated from God forever and ever, and that is really sad."

"Then I'm putting my faith in Jesus, just like Aunt C. Then someday, I will get to see her again!"

Everyone was very thankful that Aunt C knew Jesus personally before she passed away, and that made the daylong trip a little easier.

*****

We all have had someone close to us die or have experienced the death of a favorite celebrity or political figure. Regardless of whose death we have dealt with, it is never easy. The one who was always there, the one who we just talked to or spent time with, the one who loved us and whom we love is suddenly gone. This is always a sad experience but is even worse if we are uncertain if that person had a personal relationship with Jesus Christ.

As clearly stated in today's readings, everyone will die at some point; it is God's law of nature if you will. Someday we will all breathe our last breath, and our bodies will physically shut down. However, every human has an eternal entity called a soul. Our soul will either spend eternity with God or separated from him. This is why he gave us Jesus, so that we can put our faith in him and, one day, pass from this physical life into the spiritual life with him.

1. Who do you know who has passed away?
2. What was it like learning of their death?
3. Did you attend the showing and or funeral?
4. Has someone else's death helped you reflect on your own life?

Take some time, parents, to discuss with your children what death is and how we can prepare for it by knowing Jesus. Discuss, as a family, how you can properly respond to that passing of a loved one.

I know this topic is not fun to deal with, but I fully believe it is something families should openly talk about, and that, we should teach our children that death is the completion of one's physical life and the beginning of one's eternal, spiritual life.

Two Sisters and Love

Day 26
Deuteronomy 10:12–22, Proverbs 19:17,
John13:34–35, 1 John 4:7–21

"I love you, Jeepers!"

"I am well aware of that, considering how much you chase me, trying to hug me. I love you, too, of course, Creepers."

"Do you know why I love you?"

"Because I am your sister?"

"No, because God says we should love everyone! That's what Daddy told me."

"That's true. We should love everyone because God loves us, and he created everyone equally."

"Right, so I love you and Mommy and Daddy and Gwandpa and Gwandma and our aunts and uncles and our cousins and our friends—"

"So basically, you love all the people in the world."

"Yes! I love everyone!"

The two carried on through the day telling each other and their parents, "I love you."

*****

Love is incredibly powerful, but it is also very misunderstood, and the words "I love" have become much overused.

God is love—meaning, everything about his character, his decisions, and his words are love, for the good of humans who are created in his image. God does not go around saying "I love" about things or activities and so on. He reserves his love specifically for his children. Likewise, we need to be careful to only love people and not things. It's all right to thoroughly enjoy or like something, like saying, "I really like sports," but I should not love them.

To love means to wholeheartedly give our affection to and build up for the good of others. As believers, we should love all people, even when they seem to make it difficult to like them.

God tells us to show love by our actions—by sharing, giving to those in need, spending time with people who do not have family, and so on. True or godly love is always centered on the question, "What can I do to make the other person's life better?" Love is self-less, not selfish; meaning, we put others above ourselves.

There are different types of love based on the dynamics of a relationship.

Romantic love is between a husband and wife; family love is what we feel and think for our relatives; and friendship love is for everyone else.

I'm sure we have all probably heard someone say something like, "I love you, but I don't like you." I do not believe this is God's best for our love of others. We might not agree with someone in everything, but we need to do our best to live at peace with them and be a shining light of Jesus to them, even when it is challenging to get along with the other person.

1. Who are the people in your life who you love?
2. Who do you know loves you?
3. What can you do to show others the love of Christ?

As a family, come up with some practical things you can do to love each other and other people God has put in your life. (Hint: praying for someone always helps us see them the way God does, so it's probably a great place to start.)

Two Sisters and Joy

Day 27
Psalm 30, Proverbs 10:28, Isaiah 35:10,
Romans 15:13, 1 Peter 1:8–9

"Sowwy, it rained on your birthday party, Jeepers."

"It's all right, Creepers. It's not the end of the world."

"How can you still be so happy?"

"I'm happy because my joy comes from God, not stuff."

"So it doesn't matter that your party got cancelled?"

"No, because I know that God loves me, and Mom and Dad said sometimes we just have to make adjustments when things don't go the way we want. In other words, we can still be joyful even when plans change."

"Then I will be joyful with you! At least we still have yummy cake to eat!"

They went to indulge in Rachel's birthday cake but had been beat to it by their parents and their sweet tooth. The four of them sat down and enjoyed the delectable baked good together.

*****

Joy and happiness are not synonymous, contrary to popular belief. What I mean is, happiness is more of a feeling in response to something good, whereas joy is an overwhelming sense of contentment regardless of outside forces or circumstances.

Happiness says, "I will feel this way if things go well." Joy says, "I choose to stay positive and trust God no matter what."

God's joy that he gives us is complete, lacking in no way, shape, or form. We can be going through the most difficult circumstances and still experience the joy of Jesus because we know who we are in him and we know that the Father is in control.

Joy is more of a choice than a knee-jerk reaction. It is a continuous response to life.

Why was King David always praising God, even when his life was in danger? The answer lies in the fact that his joy came from knowing that God was in control and would take care of him always.

1. Who makes our joy complete?
2. Where does true joy come from?
3. Have you ever experienced something difficult but chose to remain joyful in Christ?
4. How does trusting God increase our joy?
5. How can you, as a family, encourage one another to live in the joy of Christ every day?

Be happy, but always choose God's joy no matter what.

Two Sisters and Peace

Day 28
Psalm 119:165; Proverbs 12:20; Isaiah 26:3, 12;
Romans 14:17–19; 2 Thessalonians 3:16

"Ugh, I cannot concentrate. You are being so loud, Creepers!"

"Why do you need to concentrate, Jeepers?"

"I am trying to put this puzzle together."

"What does Daddy call that when we are quiet so he can do his writing?"

"Peace. It's called peace, Ash, which is exactly what I need to complete this puzzle."

"Ah, peace! Then I will let you have peace my sister."

Ashlynn proceeded to do some sort of fairlike dance, as if she were casting a magical spell of peace over Rachel, and danced her way into her bedroom. Rachel finished the puzzle in peace.

*****

What is peace? Is it when everything is going right in your life? Or is it the overwhelming sense that God is in control, and therefore, you will not allow your faith to waiver?

In our reading, we see that God gives us his peace, and he also calls us to make peace with those around us.

Peace does not mean you will always agree with people on opinions and beliefs, but it does mean that you will love those people no matter what, and you will strive to do what is in their best interest, to bring them closer to God.

Living in peace with others means not going out of our way to bring someone down or start an argument. It also means that no matter what struggles we are facing and how bad life might seem, we know God is in control and will bring us through everything we are experiencing.

Peace is our expression of hope in Jesus, and it can be very noticeable to others.

1. Have you ever had someone ask you how you can be going through something and stay so calm and focused?
2. Were you able to tell them your peace comes from God and nothing will disrupt it?
3. What are some ways we can make the peace of God known in our lives?
4. How can you, as a family, live in God's peace and help others do the same?

May the peace of God rest on all of you!

Two Sisters and Heaven

Day 29
Isaiah 25:8–12, Ezekiel 28:24–26, Matthew
7:13–15, John 14:2–4, Hebrews 12

The sisters were playing outside on a gorgeous summer day when Rachel piped up, "Isn't this so beautiful, Creepers?"

"Yes, it is, Jeepers! All the trees are so pretty, and the sky is so blue!"

"God did such an awesome job creating this world, but Mom and Dad say it gets better in heaven!"

"Really, better than this?"

"That's right. Heaven is absolutely perfect!"

"I like the sound of that, sissy. I wonder what it will be like."

"Nobody knows every exact detail, but the Bible does give some idea of what it's like. Let's go have Mom and Dad show us the verses about heaven!"

"Okay! But we should bring them out here, and read under the tree, so we can enjoy this gorgeous day!"

They ran inside to gather their Bible and their parents.

*****

To say that God did an utterly amazing job creating the earth is a huge understatement. God himself looked at what he created and said it is good. However, when sin entered the world, the absolute perfection was lost. Now we can see the effects of sin through storms, floods, wildfires, earthquakes, and so on. This is why God has prepared a place of outright perfection in heaven for those of us who have Jesus as our Lord and Savior. Nothing on earth can even come close to comparing with the beauty and magnitude of heaven.

The Bible also states that God will create a new heaven and a new earth. Considering Satan and all of his demons will forever be locked away, sin will never again enter earth or heaven, and we will live with God in a paradise we only have some glimpses of in the Bible.

1. What do you think heaven is like?
2. Is there a loved one you are waiting to reunite with there?
3. Where is heaven?
4. Why did God create such a perfect, holy place for his children to dwell for all of eternity?

Two Sisters and the King's Return

Day 30
Matthew 24:42–44, Philippians 3:20, 1 Thessalonians
4:16–17, Hebrews 9:28, Revelation 22:20

"I'm sad that Grandpa and Grandma had to go back home, Creepers."

"Me, too, Jeepers, but Daddy said they will be back."

"That's true. I just don't like having to wait. I wonder if the disciples were sad when Jesus left."

"Where did Jesus go?"

"God brought him into heaven. The good news is that the Bible says Jesus is coming back to earth to rule as king!"

"Oh, that will be great! Mommy said that the people running the world right now are not perfect and that Jesus will make everything better."

"That's right. Jesus will bring peace and hope to everyone who puts their faith in him. He will be the greatest king we have ever seen and will eventually take us to live forever in the new heaven that God will create!"

"That is so exciting, sissy! I can't wait for Jesus to come back!"

"Neither can I!"

The sisters began cheering and singing worship songs, right there in the front yard. They were very excited by the thought of Jesus returning to earth and making everything right and perfect as God had originally intended.

*****

Here we are. We made it through an entire month of lessons from the Bible!

How sweet it is to end with the hope that is in the fact that Jesus Christ, our Lord and Savior, is coming back to the earth to restore everything onto the Father!

These verses, as well as others that you can look up as a family, are very clear that not only is Jesus coming back but that also it will not be a secret, quiet gathering. Our reading today tells us that there will be trumpets, angels, shouts of joy, and Jesus descending from the clouds on a bright, golden, fiery chariot, led by a team of snow-white horses. His return will be quite the scene and will create a great stir among the people all over the earth. Jesus will then take back what rightfully belongs to him, and the Father and will sit on his throne as the true king of the world.

We have seen how God created the world, how man brought sin into the world through disobedience, how God sent his only son to die for our sins, how God desires the church to operate, how we are to display the truth and love of Christ as a family, how God is bigger than all that we go through, and how to walk in the love, joy, and peace of Jesus no matter what. Now we are left with the assurance that Christ is, in fact, coming back to earth as king!

1. What does that mean for us, as believers?
2. Are you prepared for his return?
3. Are your friends and loved ones ready for this?
4. What can you, as a family, do while you await his second coming?

I implore each of you, whether children or adults, to stay focused. Stay ready because nobody knows exactly when Jesus is coming back, but we certainly do not want to be caught off guard and unprepared.

Writing this book has been an absolute delight, and I hope that you and your family got something good out of it.

It is my heart's desire to use this and future Jeepers and Creepers books to challenge both young and older minds in God's truth. I truly hope these stories (some true, others made up) are heartwarming and can help children relate to some of the things discussed by the sisters.

The scriptures chosen for the discussions and questions are intended to get families to explore both the Old and New Testaments, and I truly hope parents and children will take extra time looking up other verses on each subject.

Thank you so much for taking the time to work through this book together. May reading it be as much and even more of a joy and blessing to you than writing it was for me.

God bless you and your family as you search out God's Word of truth and apply it to your lives!

About the Author

Bradley J. Bidell is a thirty-four-year-old soldier in the United States Army. His two amazing daughters—Rachel, 8, and Ashlynn, 6—are the inspiration behind *Jeepers and Creepers: A Tale of Two Sisters*.

Though the sisters were born and currently reside in Wisconsin, Bradley is a native of a small town in Western New York called Albion.

Growing up, Brad and his sister attended public school and a very well rooted biblical church. Brad has always been interested in writing and felt God calling him to ministry as early as sixteen years old

Along with his profession as a full-time (active duty) soldier, Brad is in the process of earning his associate's degree in biblical studies and theology and will be attending another Christian university online in pursuit of his bachelor's degree in paralegal studies, with a minor in criminal justice.

His goal, as he continues working to become a lawyer, is to write and publish several Christian books, both fiction and nonfiction, and work in a Christian firm, defending God's sanctity of life and family.

CPSIA information can be obtained
at www.ICGtesting.com
Printed in the USA
BVHW070017040122
625366BV00006B/179

9 781638 744115